Rex Loves the Rain

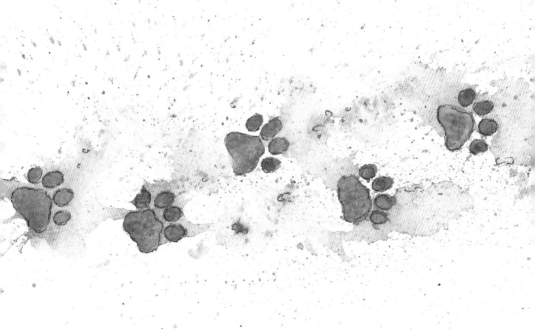

Nancy Betts

Illustrated by Peter Shaw

Rex loves the rain!

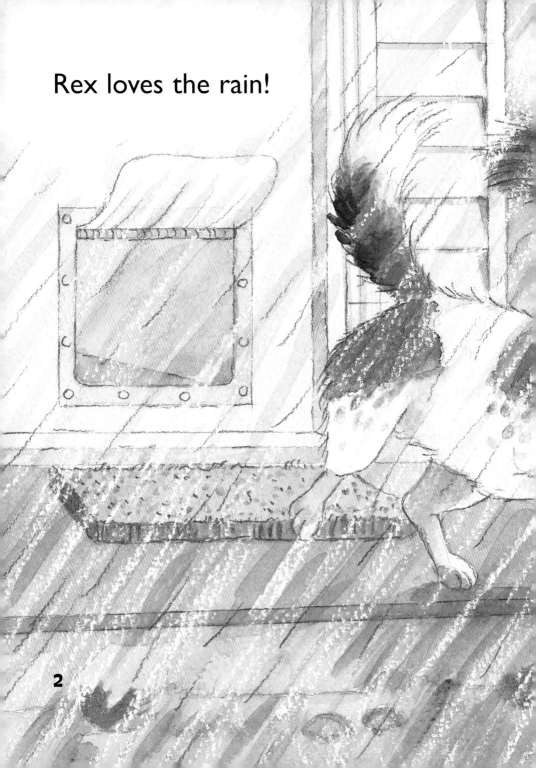

He runs outside.

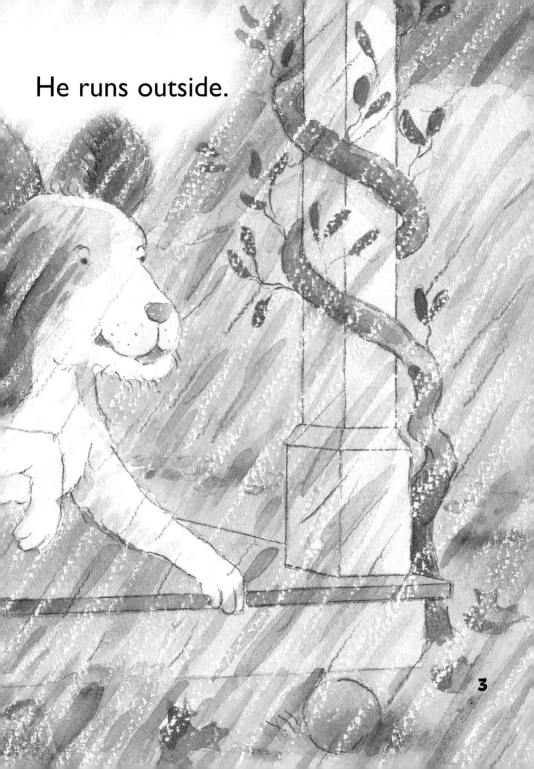

3

He plays on the wet grass.

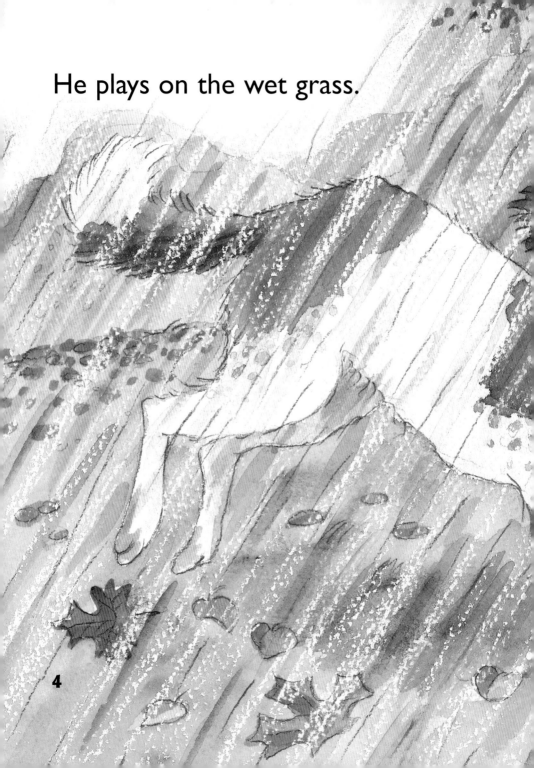

4

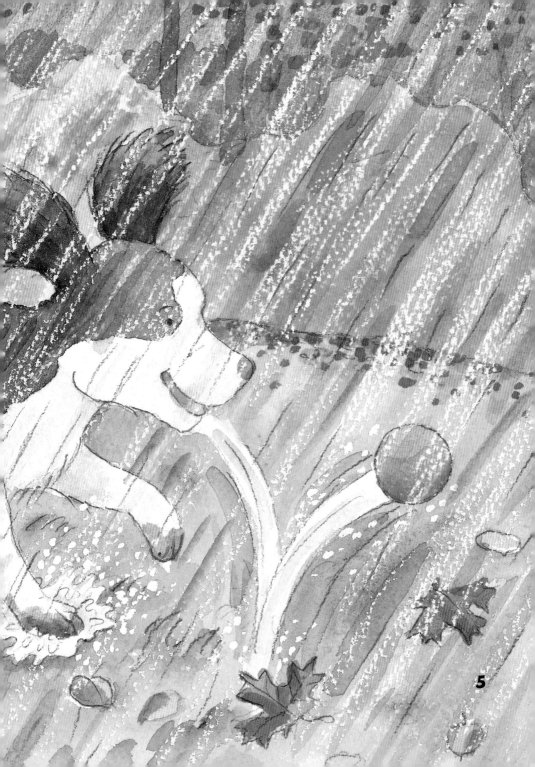

He rolls in the wet leaves.

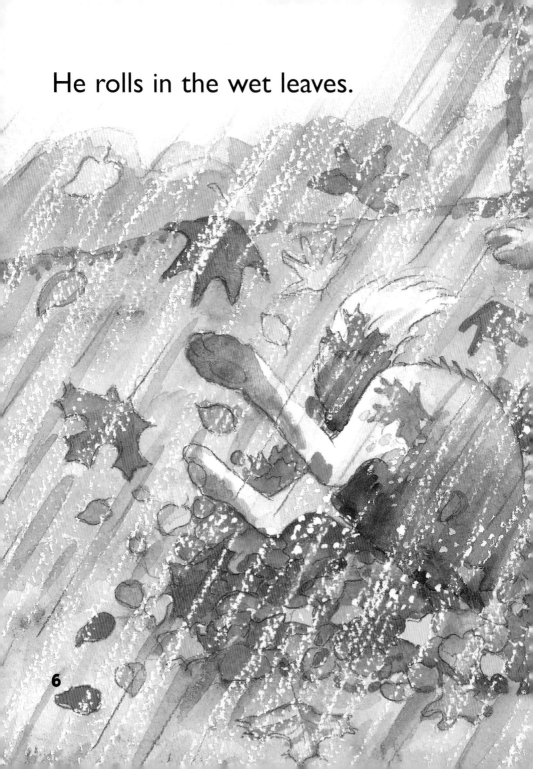

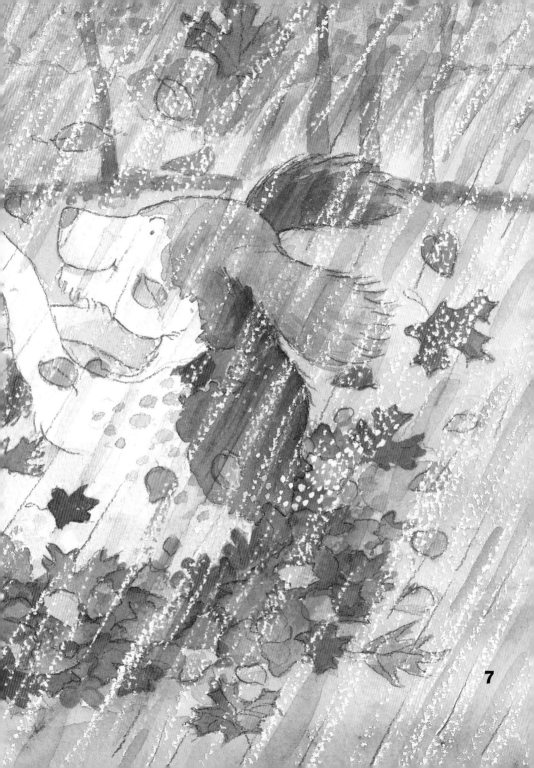

He jumps in the puddle.

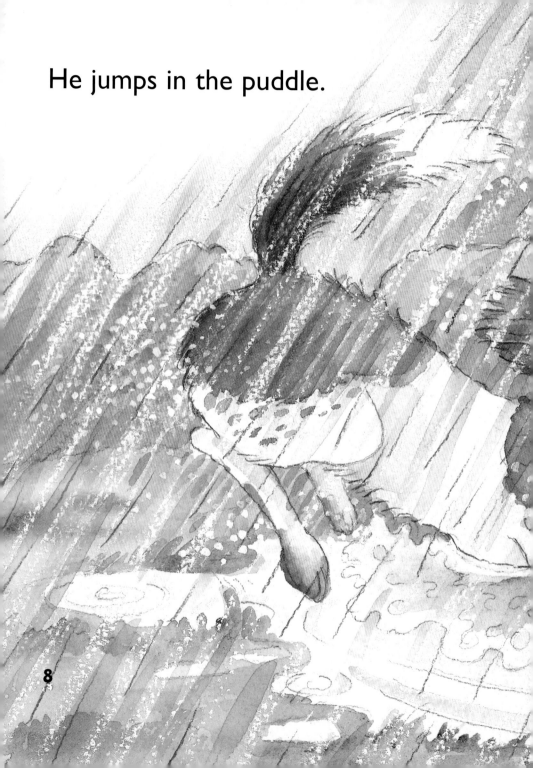

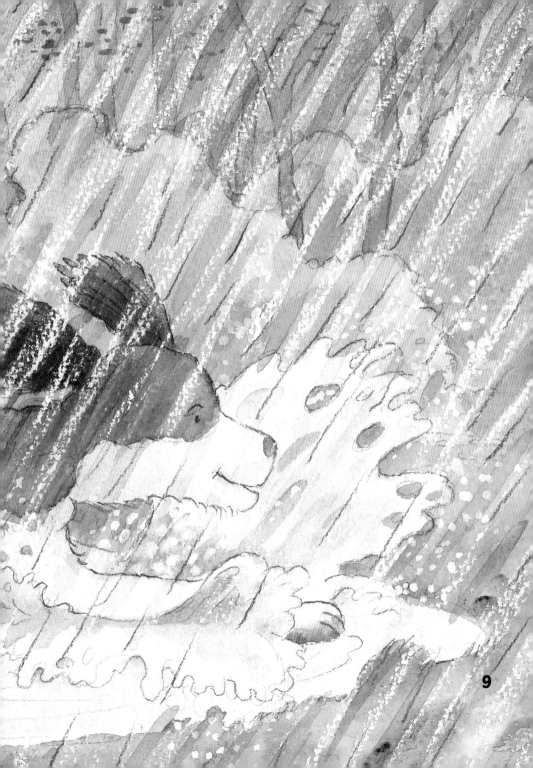

He rolls in the mud!

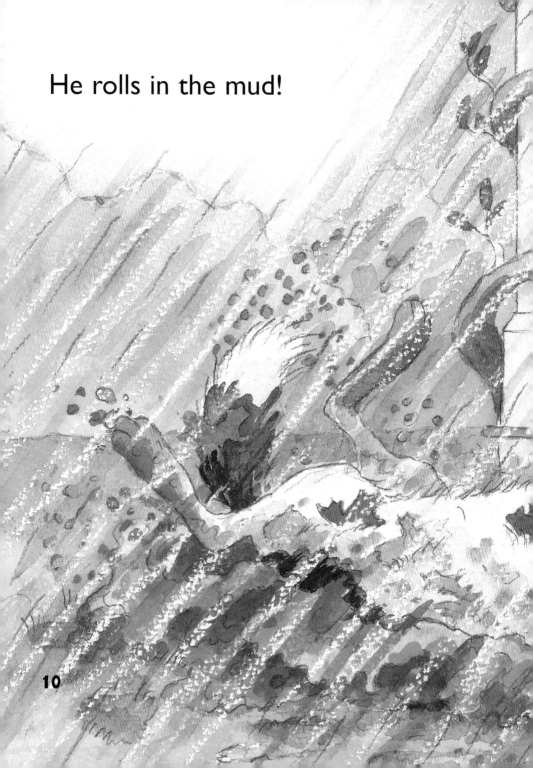

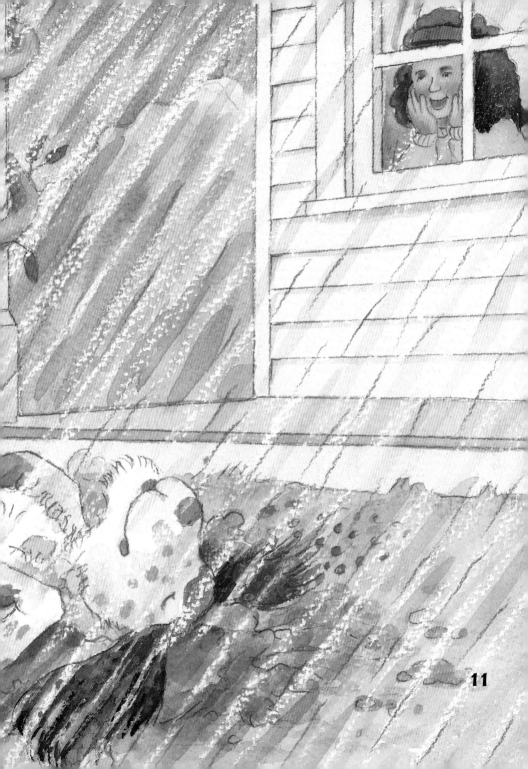

11

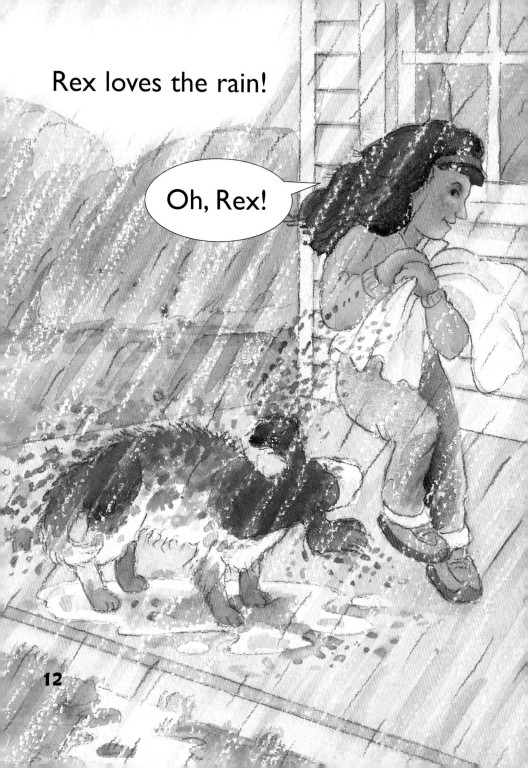